DAVID HAYES

JOHN TREVISA

TRANSLATOR AND 14TH CENTURY PRIEST TO THE BERKELEYS

Library of Congress Control Number: 2019905111

ISBN: Softcover   978-1-9845-8968-2
          Hardcover   978-1-9845-8969-9
          EBook   978-1-9845-8970-5

Print information available on the last page

Rev. date: 04/26/2019

To order additional copies of this book, contact:
Xlibris
0800-056-3182
www.xlibrispublishing.co.uk
Orders@ Xlibrispublishing.co.uk

John Trevisa

Translator and 14th Century Priest to the Berkeleys

DAVID HAYES

Introduction

John Trevisa, 'A Cornish-Speaking Father of English Prose'

In the latter half of the fourteenth century, there were great changes in the use of language in England. Richard II was the first king since the Norman conquest to use English as his preferred language. Early in the century, the vernacular of most people was English, but the educated elite and aristocracy would communicate in French, while Latin was used by the church and for general communication across Europe.

The aristocracy began to use English more and more in the latter part of the century, partly because of the intermittent wars with France. These changes also manifested themselves in written English, of which there was little in the early 1300s. Prior to and during the reign of Richard II, Chaucer and other Ricardian poets were producing works in the vernacular, the bible was being translated at Oxford University, 'Mystic' writers from eastern England were writing of their visions and of happenings in everyday life, and chroniclers were using English to record the events of the time. The greatest amount of written English from this period, however, came from the Cornishman John Trevisa. Sponsored by Lord Berkeley, he translated from Latin two encyclopaedias and other works of secular polemic and at the same time added writings and comments of his own, which offer a valuable insight into the state of the language in use at that time. He thus had a large influence on standardising the type of English we use today.

John Trevisa was probably born in St Enoder in Cornwall around 1342 and educated at Glasney Collegiate before arriving at Oxford University in 1362. He was ordained a priest in 1370, became vicar of Berkeley in 1374, and later became chaplain to Lord Berkeley. Latterly, he had some fifteen or so other clergy under his charge. Most of his translations were done from the 1380s. He died about 1402 and is said to be buried in Berkeley church.

Much of the research into the life of John Trevisa was undertaken by the American David Fowler (1921–2007). David Fowler lived in Cornwall and Oxford for a while and, together with his two daughters, learned to speak Cornish.

Little is known of Trevisa's day-to-day life, so this booklet simply describes the events at places he was known to be habiting, his two sponsors, and his translations.

St Enoder

Trevisa's date of birth can be approximately dated at 1342 by assuming he would be about nineteen at his known date of entry to Oxford. And he was, from the evidence, in all probability, born at St Enoder in Cornwall.

Muniments in Berkeley Castle show that in the 1300s, the lords of Berkeley owned and collected rent from the manor of Tygembreth, which held land at Trevessa and Penscawen; both are still in the parish of St Enoder. The name Trevisa can be found in the records of the gentry living in St Enoder and neighbouring Mitchel in the 1300s.

It is known that Lord Thomas III of Berkeley travelled widely and would sometimes visit his manors. He was also generous in giving to chantries and in providing education for the young. So, it is likely that, having met or become aware of a talented young son of one of his tenants, he would have been willing to help by sponsoring his education. In the case of John Trevisa, that education would have been at Glasney Collegiate, in Penryn.

The parish of St Enoder, with its fertile agricultural land and location on the main pilgrim's route to St Michael's Mount, was once one of the richest in Cornwall. Today, it is bypassed by the A30, but its church tower is clearly visible from the road. In 1270, the parish, together with thirteen other parishes, was appropriated by Glasney College and required to pay taxes to help with the upkeep of the college. The college appointed a canon responsible for St Enoder, and he designated a vicar to live and work in the parish. The taxes paid to Glasney and Rome would be a considerable burden, and following the loss of workers after the plague of 1349, the church fell into disrepair.

Most of the church had to be rebuilt after Trevisa's time, but a Norman font which could have been used for his baptism remains. Some carvings on the pews are thought to date from the thirteenth century.

Medieval font and carved pews in St Enoder Church.

GLASNEY COLLEGE

The Collegiate College of St Thomas, also referred to as Glasney College, was founded by Bishop Walter Bronescombe of Exeter in 1264, following a visit to Germany. He intended it to be 'a powerful influence for good in the Cornish church'. He also needed it as a place where he could stay and as an administrative centre for the often hostile Cornish populous. The project had the support of Richard, Earl of Cornwall, King Henry III's very affluent brother, who had already built Tintagel Castle. He also succeeded in his ambition to become Holy Roman Emperor.

The design of the college was similar to Exeter Cathedral but scaled to two-thirds its size, and with three additional towers for the defence of the port of Penryn. Like Exeter, it was built with Devon Beer stone, a fine, creamy limestone with excellent masonry properties, which had been heavily quarried near the village of Beer. This stone was reputedly a favourite of Julius Caesar.

Collegiate became the centre of ecclesiastic power in Cornwall and offered the most esteemed educational opportunities to its students. Consequently, students like John Trevisa, who were academically capable and had the financial means, were able to continue their education by going from Glasney on to Oxford University.

In Trevisa's time, Bishop John Grandisson (1327–1369) of Exeter brought many improvements to the college. Bishop Grandisson is famous for the many changes he made to Exeter Cathedral, which can still be seen today.

Power within the college was structured with one provost, and beneath him served twelve secular canons. Income was derived from its fourteen appropriated parishes, with St Enoder being one of the richest of these. Amongst other things, this income would have been used to support the fifty to seventy residents on site in the fourteenth century.

In this period, the so-called miracle plays were produced in the Cornish language and enacted at the college and at *plen an gwary* sites in West Cornwall. These served to entertain and educate the mostly monoglot populace about the Bible stories. In the college, all business and church matters would be conducted in Latin, but the common vernacular was Cornish.

The demise of this once-proud Cornish institution came at the hands of Henry VIII, who from 1536 to 1541, ordered the dissolution of the monasteries and other religious houses. It was a radical move, as it was estimated that one in fifty adult males lived in religious orders at the time. Glasney survived a little longer than many but was finally sold and dismantled in 1548.

All that remains is an ivy-covered wall and part of a small archway, although some original stones can be found in nearby buildings as well as in Penryn Museum. Recent excavation works have allowed a team to map out the original position of the walls.

Some college remains in the area.

Carved stone
fragments from the
Glasney site

Stone erected by Friends of Glasney College on the excavated site

OXFORD UNIVERSITY

Trevisa states that Oxford was a seat of learning since the time of King Alfred. Although this remark cannot be substantiated, the university is, however, one of the oldest in the world and seems to have evolved in the twelfth century.

The bishop of Exeter and chancellor to Edward II, Walter Stapledon, together with his brother Richard, founded Stapledon Hall at Oxford in 1312 for students of the Exeter diocese. The hall held about twelve students, with four or so from Cornwall. In 1327, Stapledon, an unpopular minister, and his brother were killed by a mob when they remained in London after Edward II was forced to flee. Their bodies were later returned and interred in Exeter Cathedral.

Stapledon Hall, later to be called Exeter College, housed several notable Cornishmen prior to the arrival of Trevisa, and some may have influenced his perspective.

Robert Tresillian, a Cornish JP, was appointed lord chief justice by King Richard. He was involved in the ruthless suppression after the peasants' revolt in 1381. When the Lords Appellant, a group of nobles who revolted against the king's rule, took control of the country between 1386 and 1388, Tresillian became subject of their revenge during the 'merciless Parliament'. Ignoring the laws of sanctuary, he was seized, dragged out of Westminster, and hanged, despite pleas for his life from King Richard and the queen.

Ralph de Tremur, who was said to be fluent in Cornish, English, French, and Latin, was given a benefice in the parish of Warleggan, but he rarely put in an appearance there. He spent most of his time preaching in Oxford and the south-west. His radical views may have influenced the ideas of the famed reformer John Wycliffe. Eventually, his preaching was tolerated no longer, and he was summoned to appear before Bishop Grandisson of Exeter, who then fulminated against him from the pulpit.

William de Polmorva became chancellor of Oxford University in 1350 and was later confessor to Edward III's wife, Phillipa.

Trevisa also names two other Cornish graduates, Richard Pencriche and John Cornwall, teachers in the Oxford area who used English instead of French to teach grammar to children.

In Oxford, for many years, there were conflicts between town and gown, which reached a climax six years before Trevisa's arrival, when a riot in the town led to the defeat of the students, who suffered sixty-three deaths. On appeal, the king sided with the students, granting protection and privileges. He fined the town, requiring it make an annual payment to the university. This continued until the 1800s.

John Trevisa began his time at Exeter College Oxford in January 1362, an unusual time of year, but this may have been connected to the death of his putative sponsor, Thomas Berkeley, late in 1361. After seven years, which was typical for that era, he obtained his master of arts, and in 1369, he moved to Queen's College to pursue his studies for a doctorate. He transferred with three others from Exeter College, including Nicholas Hereford, a known contributor to the Bible translation.

At that time, a doctor of arts degree would have taken ten years. We know that Trevisa was there and retained rooms, intermittently, for a further sixteen years, but it is unclear whether he completed his doctorate in this time. It is clear the doctorate was not his only pursuit. In 1370, he was ordained as a priest, and the evidence suggests that he became vicar of Berkeley around 1374.

In 1376, Trevisa was involved in the 'trouble at Quenehaelle (Queen's Hall)'. Queen's Hall was founded for students from northern counties, but there had been an influx of six students from Exeter College, and the northerners had become outnumbered. Thomas Carlisle, a northerner, was appointed provost, but the southerners wanted their man. A dispute ensued, and eventually it was necessary to obtain an order from King Edward, commanding observance of the constitution. The northerners had won, but anticipating this adverse decision, the southerners left, taking with them the college seal and other items which enabled them to continue their studies. Various writs naming Trevisa and others and court cases followed. The problem dragged on for four years before it seems to have been resolved amicably.

Of particular interest to students now is a list of the twenty-four books that were taken and later returned. They included the *Polychronicon* (which Trevisa later translated), a Bible, various commentaries on sections of the Bible, and a book of Latin grammar.

Trevisa was at Queen's during the controversy of 1382. At that time, Oxford was considered a hotbed of religious radical reform, or according to Archbishop Courtenay, a 'nurse of heresies', with John Wycliffe and his followers considered to be the cause. The archbishop convened a meeting consisting mostly of friars, the majority of whom he had selected. Called the Blackfriars Council, its purpose was to suppress the ideas of these dissidents. The council produced a list of condemnations of the twenty-four conclusions attributable to Wycliffe and ordered that this list be read out at Oxford prior to a sermon from Nicholas Hereford. The university chancellor, however, wishing to retain the independence of the university and protect the free speech of its members, refused this outside interference. The chancellor and others were subsequently summoned to see the archbishop and forced to back down.

Archbishop Courtenay visited the university in November 1382. Those who had been supporters of Wycliffe were obliged to recant publically, and thereafter, any critic of the church would be condemned as a heretic. We can only surmise that Trevisa would have been dismayed by all these events. He had been a friend of Wycliffe and would likely have blamed the friars for the silencing of Wycliffe's views. Interestingly, one of Trevisa's later translations was of a sermon by Richard FitzRalph in which he attacked the friars. Arguments about the amount of free speech allowable continue to this day.

THE LORDS OF BERKELEY

The beautifully preserved walls of Berkeley Castle, one of the Marcher castles, can be found at the edge of the small town of Berkeley in Gloucestershire. Its origins were as a motte-and-bailey castle constructed around 1067 by William FitzOsbern, a close counsellor of William the Conqueror, but in 1152, the feudal barony of Berkeley was handed to Robert Fitzharding, who became the founder of the Berkeley family and began the construction of today's castle. Robert, the first Lord Berkeley, also founded St Augustine Abbey in Bristol, which was later to become Bristol Cathedral and is the burial place of some of the Berkeley lords. The Berkeley family continue to reside in the building to this day.

In the middle ages, the Berkeley family were generally loyal to the king and fought in most of the battles against the Scottish and French armies. On the two occasions, when they quarrelled with the monarch towards the end of the reigns of both Edward II and Richard II, they played a contributing role in both the kings' downfalls.

In the fourteenth century, Maurice Berkeley III supported Roger Mortimer in the 'Despenser War'. This led to both he and his son being imprisoned by Edward II in Wallingford prison. He died in incarceration in 1326, but his son Thomas III managed to escape.

Thomas III was a close friend of the influential Roger Mortimer and later married his daughter Margaret. Roger Mortimer also had a feud with Edward II and was imprisoned, but he escaped and fled to France, where he was later joined by Edward's queen consort Isabella. Together they lead a revolt to depose the king. They ruled as regents through the authority of Isabella's son Edward III. After Edward II's capture by Mortimer's army, he was initially held in Kenilworth Castle, and later, Thomas Berkeley was given the responsibility of holding him prisoner in Berkeley Castle. The room where he was held and allegedly killed is exhibited to visitors today. Thomas's role in this event remains an enigma. He was indicted for allowing Edward's alleged murder, but at a trial by his peers, he gave the implausible response that he was ill on the day and knew nothing about it. Whereas others who were also involved were pursued and killed, he was allowed to go free and was pardoned by Edward III several years later. Historians are now divided in their opinion as to whether Edward II really did die in Berkeley Castle or whether he escaped, fled to Corfe Castle, and later his way to a monastery in Pavia Italy via Ireland and Avignon. Evidence for this latter theory comes from a number of strange circumstances and from a description in the more recently discovered de Fieschi letter, which was written to Edward III by the Genoese priest Manuele de Fieschi. Maybe someday, DNA analysis of the body in Edward II's tomb in Gloucester Cathedral will give an answer.

Apart from his role in the power dispute of the crown, Thomas III travelled widely, and this probably included visits to his manors in Cornwall. He gave generously to chantries and sponsored the education of students. It was this same Thomas Berkeley III that we presume funded the young John Trevisa from the time of his move to Glasney College. In 1340s, Thomas oversaw significant expansion to the castle with a number of constructions that can be seen today: Thorpe's tower, the inner gatehouse, and other buildings of the inner bailey.

Thomas Berkeley III's family were involved in the Glasney-Exeter-Oxford connections, which have already been mentioned. His uncle James held a short-term tenure as bishop of Exeter following the murder of Bishop Walter Stapledon, and three brothers each played a role in the network. Peter was a canon of Glasney (1331–1334), Sir Maurice was able to persuade King Edward III to allow certain Glasney canons to retain their benefices, and Eudo completed his studies at Oxford University.

After the death of his wife, Margaret, Thomas III married the widowed Katharine de Clevedon and had a further six children. At the age of 61, he was still able to fight at Poitiers, but he died five years later, in 1361, and was interred in St Mary's Church, Berkeley. Katharine continued to be an active member of society, founding a chantry and a grammar school at

Wooton. She outlived her husband by twenty-five years before she finally joined him in their large tomb, which occupies a prominent position to the side of the altar.

Maurice IV succeeded his father as heir to the Berkeley estate in 1361, having married Elizabeth Despenser when both were 8 years old. Elizabeth was a daughter of Hugh Despenser the Younger, the avaricious friend of Edward II and long time enemy of the Berkeley family. Hugh Despenser was brutally executed a year after Elizabeth's birth, when Roger Mortimer and Queen Isabella seized power. Maurice fought at Crecy and later at Poitiers, where he was wounded and captured, returning home only after his ransom had been paid. In 1365, Edward III appointed him commissioner of St Augustine Priory in Bristol to help resolve its financial problems. He held the tenure of Berkeley Estates for only seven years before dying in 1368, according to the Chronicler Froissart, of the effects of his war injuries.

Thomas IV, his son, was married to Margaret de Lisle when he was 14 and she was only 7. They did not meet, however, until several years later. This marriage added to his already considerable wealth. In 1368, he inherited the title at the young age of 16 years, and on inheritance, he immediately became one of the seventy-five most powerful magnates in the country, being required to attend Parliament when necessary. King Richard succeeded his grandfather at the age of 10 in 1377, after the deaths of both his father, the 'Black Prince', and his elder brother, Edward of Angouleme. Richard II visited Berkeley in 1386, and although Thomas disapproved of many of the king's actions, he was able to distance himself from the lords appellant when they revolted and took control of the government from 1386 to 1388, and thus he managed to escape from Richard's vindictive revenge some ten years later. He did, however, alienate himself from Richard by arranging the marriage of his only daughter to Richard Beauchamp, son of the Earl of Warwick, an appellant lord who was later imprisoned by King Richard.

In 1399, when Richard II sailed to Ireland, he left his uncle, Edmund of Langley, the duke of York, as guardian of the realm. Henry Bolingbroke, Richard's first cousin, who had taken part in the lord appellant's rebellion against him and was later exiled, took the opportunity to re-enter the country. Gathering forces, he met up with the duke of York at

Berkeley Castle, where the duke was persuaded not to use his army to oppose the invasion of Henry Bolingbroke. This, in effect, sealed Richard's fate.

In Shakespeare's Richard II, *The Duke of York says,*

'It may be I will go with you:-but yet I'll pause; For I am loth to break our country's laws,

Nor friends nor foes, to me welcome you are: Things past redress are now with me past care.

Thomas Berkeley was appointed as one of the commissioners who arranged for the deposition of Richard, and when Henry took the throne, Thomas became a member of the privy council. He supplied ships and commanded the western fleet and arranged to bring Joan, Henry IV's new bride, from Brittany.

Thomas Berkeley IV continued the family interest in education, and it is to him that we are indebted for the development of the English language. He invested in literature on an unprecedented scale, sponsoring his Chaplain John Trevisa to undertake a vast output of translations. Having extensive business interests in wool and shipping, he was required to visit London frequently, where he owned property (now Berkeley Square). This gave him the opportunity to arrange for copies of Trevisa's translations to be made and sold to other interested parties. Thomas Berkeley did not only use John Trevisa for his promotion of written vernacular; he had acquired an ornate psalter written in English by the mystic writer Richard Rolle, and after Trevisa's demise, he sponsored an English translation of a military treatise by the Roman Vegetius. His daughter Elizabeth continued the family interest and also commissioned a number of translations in English.

Thomas never remarried after his wife Margaret died in 1393, and so, when he died in 1417, there was no direct heir. This caused a family feud and legal disputes about the inheritance which lasted over one hundred years.

Berkeley Family Tree

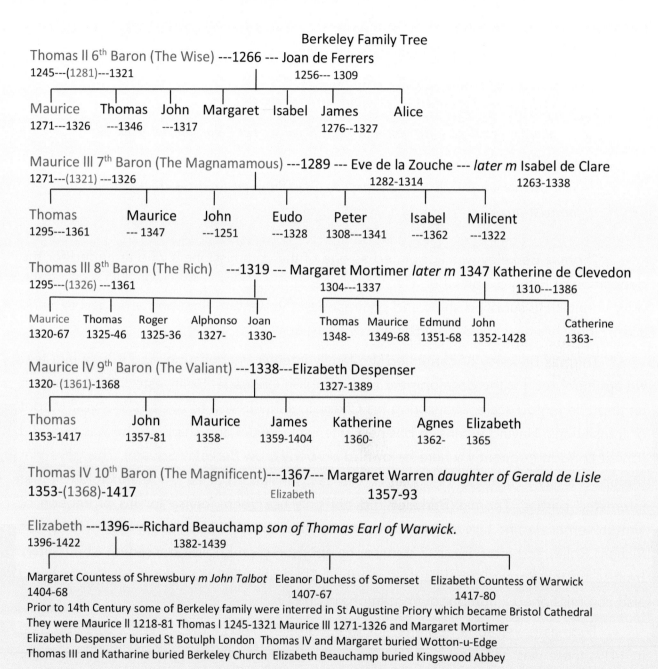

Thomas II 6th Baron (The Wise) ---1266--- **Joan de Ferrers**
1245---(1281)---1321   1256--- 1309

Maurice	Thomas	John	Margaret	Isabel	James	Alice
1271---1326	---1346	---1317			1276--1327	

Maurice III 7th Baron (The Magnamamous) ---1289--- **Eve de la Zouche** --- *later m* Isabel de Clare
1271---(1321)---1326   1282-1314   1263-1338

Thomas	Maurice	John	Eudo	Peter	Isabel	Milicent
1295---1361	--- 1347	---1251	---1328	1308---1341	---1362	---1322

Thomas III 8th Baron (The Rich) ---1319--- **Margaret Mortimer** *later m* 1347 Katherine de Clevedon
1295---(1326)---1361   1304---1337   1310---1386

Maurice	Thomas	Roger	Alphonso	Joan	Thomas	Maurice	Edmund	John	Catherine
1320-67	1325-46	1325-36	1327-	1330-	1348-	1349-68	1351-68	1352-1428	1363-

Maurice IV 9th Baron (The Valiant) ---1338---**Elizabeth Despenser**
1320- (1361)-1368   1327-1389

Thomas	John	Maurice	James	Katherine	Agnes	Elizabeth
1353-1417	1357-81	1358-	1359-1404	1360-	1362-	1365

Thomas IV 10th Baron (The Magnificent)---1367--- **Margaret Warren** *daughter of Gerald de Lisle*
1353-(1368)-1417   Elizabeth   1357-93

Elizabeth ---1396---**Richard Beauchamp** *son of Thomas Earl of Warwick.*
1396-1422   1382-1439

Margaret Countess of Shrewsbury *m John Talbot*	Eleanor Duchess of Somerset	Elizabeth Countess of Warwick
1404-68	1407-67	1417-80

Prior to 14th Century some of Berkeley family were interred in St Augustine Priory which became Bristol Cathedral
They were Maurice II 1218-81 Thomas I 1245-1321 Maurice III 1271-1326 and Margaret Mortimer
Elizabeth Despenser buried St Botulph London Thomas IV and Margaret buried Wotton-u-Edge
Thomas III and Katharine buried Berkeley Church Elizabeth Beauchamp buried Kingswood Abbey

Tomb of Thomas III and Katharine in Berkeley church.

Tomb of Thomas IV and Margaret in Wooton under Edge Church.

WESTBURY-ON-TRYM

Westbury-on-Trym is today a suburb of Bristol, but in the fourteenth century, when Bristol was a small village, it had a collegiate church of growing importance with canons who went onto the highest offices.

In 1362, the famous reformer John Wycliffe was appointed canon and held office there until his death in 1384. He seems, however, to have rarely visited. The bishop of Worcester found the church to be in a neglected state and that Wycliffe had failed to provide a chaplain in his absence. All rather strange, because Wycliffe preached against church hierarchy receiving benefices without fulfilling their duties.

Following Wycliffe's death, it seems that the Dean of Westbury tried to impede Trevisa's installation as a Canon at Westbury, which had a prebend at Woodbury just south of Berkeley. This post would have given Trevisa a source of income, money he needed to pay for a priest and support for carrying out his duties as chaplain to Lord Berkeley. The dean wanted to give the prebend to his own candidate.

In 1388, Trevisa with a band of armed men broke into the dean's chamber, abducted, beat, and imprisoned the dean. A further similar attack was carried out again nine months later. There is opposing evidence showing that the dean's factions attacked and occupied Woodbury. This dispute was referred to King Richard. It may be that at this stage, the king, having his own problems, wished to keep the influential Lord Berkeley on his side. We do not know his verdict, but Trevisa did continue to be a canon of Westbury. Correspondence from this case in Norman French and English translation can be found in David Fowler's book.

This episode, together with his expulsion from Queen's College Oxford, show a rather belligerent side to Trevisa's nature.

WRITINGS AND TRANSLATIONS

'Dialogue between a Lord and a Clerk' and 'Epistle'

The 'Dialogue' was written by Trevisa as a means of explaining his reasons for making the translations from Latin, and it is invaluable for helping us to understand the thinking at that time about the use of written English. It was written about 1385–1387, and it prefaces six of the fourteen copies of the *Polychronicon*, now extant and whose completion date is written as 1387.

The arguments are given as a dialogue between a lord, representing Lord Berkeley, and a clerk, representing Trevisa. In this case, it is the lord who takes the peremptory role addressing the clerk as 'thou', whilst the clerk, who uses the more respectful 'ye', poses the questions and has the more naive arguments. This was a reversal of the usual form for this type of debate, where the clerk is given the more knowledgeable role.

The lord points out that communication can fail when many languages are used ('the curse of Babel') and that Latin had resolved this problem, helping to exchange ideas, but now, it was being abused by the clergy for their own ends, and English was now adequate for communication and book learning. The clerk says that the people who would want to read the *Polychronicon* would know Latin, but the lord responds by saying that some would not have Latin versions or, like himself, would know some Latin but find English easier.

Much of the debate concerns the question, pertinent at the time, of translation of the Bible. The church at this time had not condemned translations, but they were considered to be subversive and a threat to the church's authority. The clerk proffers the view that 'many say the Holy Writ should not be translated', to which the lord counters that the Holy Writ was itself a translation of Hebrew into Greek and then into Latin by St Jerome, and that parts had already been translated. He goes on to list King Alfred, Bishop Wyrfryth, and the monks Caedmon and Bede. The lord also mentions the inscriptions from the Book of Revelation on the chapel (now the morning room) in Berkeley Castle in Latin and French. Today, sadly, these are hardly readable.

In the 'Epistle', Trevisa calls himself priest and beadsman to Lord Berkeley and explains how he did the translation for him sometimes word for word and sometimes more liberally but always trying to preserve the true meaning.

The Polychronicon

The *Polychronicon*, or 'Chronicles of Time', was written in Latin by Ranulf Higden, a Benedictine monk of St Werberg Chester. At the time, it was the most complete history of the world. It is divided into seven ages, starting from Creation and ending around 1340.

John Trevisa finished translating the work into English in 1387. The book was copied around the Gloucester area and was taken to London and promoted by Thomas Berkeley. In London, further copies were made. These books were copied on rich vellum, indicating a market for the educated aristocracy. One copy of interest is embossed with Warwick coat of arms and was a gift from Lord Berkeley to his son-in-law Henry Beauchamp, Earl of Warwick.

A further translation of the Latin original was made fifty years later and at the end of the fifteenth century. William Caxton printed the Trevisa version and brought the history up to date with an eighth part. These two versions are useful to scholars studying the change in the English language over the years. Differences between copies of the Trevisa version made in the London and Gloucester Scriptoria help to indicate the different dialogues that were in use at that time.

The *Polychronicon* is also interesting because Trevisa adds several notes of his own to the translation. In one instance, Higden says that French is the dominant language in schools, but Trevisa writes that since the plague, all teaching in grammar schools is now in English. He mentions two Cornishmen: John Cornwall, a master of grammar, and Richard Pencrich, who have enabled the children of their schools to leave French and to construe and learn English, thus enabling them to learn their grammar in less time. In another part, Higden says that England has thirty-six shires apart from Cornwall. Trevisa writes that it must be part of England and is adamant that Cornwall is one of the main parts of Britain.

Higden says that King Edgar founded monasteries but the clerks and vicars became corrupt and had to be replaced by monks; however, Trevisa adds that now 'the monks are worst of all for they be too rich', and he quotes from Jerome, that since the holy church has increased in possessions, it has decreased in virtues, and he adds that this superfluity of possessions should be given to those that need it. His views on monasteries may have influenced Thomas IV of Berkeley, who, unlike Thomas III, failed to establish a single monastic foundation.

FitzRalph's Defensio Curatorum

Trevisa translated this sermon by FitzRalph from Latin to allow the work to have a wider vernacular debate.

(1299–1360 Richard FitzRalph) was an Anglo Irishman. He was an Oxford graduate who became chancellor of the university in 1332 and bishop of Armagh in 1347. Whilst at Oxford, he encountered controversy with the friars. He was famous for his sermons written in Latin preaching against the laxity in the church and against corruption of mendicant friars. He made four visits to the pope in Avignon. He died in Rome but was buried in Dundalk.

'Defensio Curatorum' was delivered in 1357 to the pope and cardinals. In it, he argued that mendicant friars are unnecessary, are damaging to parish priests, and use confessions only for financial reward to themselves. He advocated abolishing all mendicant friars.

Trevisa, as a parish priest, would no doubt have felt some sympathy for these sentiments, but in this translation, he adds no comments of his own. His experiences at Oxford no doubt contributed to his reasons for making this translation.

This work was widely distributed and eighty-four of the documents are still extant.

Dispute between Knight and Clerk

The authorship of this dialogue is not known, but William of Okham is the favoured choice. It is about the conflicts between Phillip IV of France and the pope on the rights of a king to tax the clergy.

Phillip IV (Le Bel) was a profligate king who wished to increase his power in Europe and needed more money for the defence of the realm and for his wars against the English and the county of Flanders. The pope, Boniface VIII, adopted a hard line until his death in 1303, saying that the king had no right to tax the church. The arguments split Europe, with many influential people taking opposing views. A later French pope, Clement V, was more amenable to Philip's wishes and relocated the official seat of the papacy from Rome to Avignon in 1307. Without the papal condemnation, Philip was able to expel Jews from his country, to imprison, torture, and slaughter the Templars, and to seize all their considerable assets.

The treatise takes the form of a debate between a knight who speaks for the king and a clerk who speaks for the church of Pope Benedict's time. Both give sound reasons for their point of view. The knight describes the scenario in which, because the church would not help with taxes, the country could be overrun by its enemies and the church's wealth would then be taken anyway.

This conflict was hotly debated in many countries and in particular in Oxford in Wycliffe's time, so Trevisa would have been well aware of the various arguments. In his translation, he amends the meaning of the Latin slightly in accordance with his views, and he gives the opinion that some church reform is necessary.

Rule of Princes

'De Regimine Principum' was written by Giles of Rome and again concerns Philip IV 'Le Bel' of France. Giles had been tutor to the young king but had fallen out of favour and later opposed the king's views.

Giles argued that the power of the king must be restrained by the church, and he gives a protocol for a prince's good behaviour.

This work is in three parts and is based on the ideas of Aristotle. The parts concern 'the self', 'the household', and 'the realm'. It was one of the most successful attempts at mediating Aristotle's philosophy and is still conserved in more than three hundred manuscripts in the original Latin and in other vernaculars.

There is, however, only one extant translation of this lengthy work by Trevisa. It is beautifully illustrated and is held in the Bodleian library. Other copies are mentioned in fifteenth-century wills, but it probably had a limited circulation. We do not know why Thomas Berkeley wanted this translation. It may have been meant for the young wayward King Richard, but Richard's tutor, Simon Burley, already had a French version, or it could also have been intended for young Henry V.

Bartholemew's 'The Properties of Things'

Bartholemew de Glanville was an English Franciscan who had travelled in Europe and studied in Oxford and Paris. He completed his scientific encyclopaedia *De Proprietibus Rerum* in 1245. Trevisa dates the completion of his four-volume translation at Berkeley as the sixth day of February 1398. There are eight copies still in existence. The work was put into print in 1495, and a further printed version was made as recently as 1992.

The Gospel of Nicodemus

Sadly, we do not know when or why Trevisa translated this book, but a note made about 1425 in one of the three existing copies says that the translation 'out of latyn into englisshe laboured by maystere Johan Trevysa Doctour in theologye at the instaunce of Thomae some tyme lord of Berkley'. David Fowler gives his reasons as to why he considers it to be one of Trevisa's earliest works.

The gospel of Nicodemus has never been accepted into the church canon and is of doubtful authenticity. It was supposedly written by Nicodemus, a disciple of Christ, but scholars think it was written some four hundred years later in order to add authenticity to the other gospels. The book is in two sections describing the Passion and the Resurrection of Christ, with an additional part concerning Christ's descent into hell. In the latter, two types of hell are described, one for the permanently damned and one for those who had lived before the time of Christ and were awaiting his arrival. Trevisa seems to have favoured this scenario, as he quotes it in one of the many notes he added to the Polychronicon. In this case, it was in a comment he made following the description of the Northumbrian king Edwin's soul being delivered from hell by the prayers of St Dunstan.

The Bible

Parts of the Bible have been translated into English from the time of King Alfred, but a fuller translation of both Testaments was undertaken in Oxford by John Wycliffe and his associates, who would have included John Trevisa. This Bible is generally called the Wycliffe

Bible, although it has been shown that there are two versions, now called Wycliffe A and Wycliffe B. The Wycliffe A is a more literal translation in accordance with Wycliffe's view that the sacred text should not be altered. Wycliffe B is a freer translation with similarities to Trevisa's other works.

The authorship of this B version is still hotly debated. Trevisa, as translator, was acknowledged by the scholar and historian John Bale (1495–1563) and later by the printer William Caxton (1422–1491). The preface to the King James Bible also cites Trevisa as the translator. The B version did not appear until 1388 after Wycliffe's death, and eight years after the A version, it shows advancement in the use of English. One passage about the Creation in Wycliffe B is very similar to the one in the Polychronicon, which was finished in 1387.

Attitudes to the translation of the Bible were, however, changing. Wycliffe had originally been encouraged to undertake the work, but after the peasants' revolt of 1381, it was considered to be subversive. Wycliffe was summoned to appear before Archbishop Courtney on a charge of heresy, but Wycliffe had friends in high places, including King Richard's wife and mother and John of Gaunt, so he was able to acquit himself.

The church enjoyed the ability to interpret the Bible to the laypeople as they saw fit and thus could become wealthy by charging for indulgencies. The pope decreed that translation of the Bible into any vernacular was prohibited.

When Henry IV usurped the throne he reinstated Archbishop Arundel and an even more hard line, than had been the case under Archbishop Courtenay, was taken, so that even possession of a Bible was considered a heresy punishable by burning. Wycliffe had already died, but years later, his bones were disinterred and burnt.

Surprisingly, many of these early Bibles have survived, but it was to be over one hundred years before William Tyndale's Bibles, this time translated from the Greek and Hebrew, could be smuggled into Britain.

King Richard's first wife, Anne of Bohemia, had helped foster links between Oxford and Prague, so Wycliffe's works came to the attention of a group of students there. One Jan Hus later translated the Bible into Czech and modernised the Czech language. He was also burnt at the stake as a heretic, but after his death, the 'Hussite' movement grew in strength and defeated several crusades against it from Rome.

Not surprisingly, Trevisa seems to have been quiet about his part in the translation of the Bible, but hints can be found in his works.

Piers Plowman

This long allegorical poem was written using alliterative lines. It follows the narrator in his quest for salvation, but it is also a satire on corruption in the church.

The work exists in fifty texts all differ slightly. They are classified into three main texts, called A, B, and C. The 'A' text is generally attributed to William Langland, but scholars argue as to whether Langland or others wrote the later versions. David Fowler put forward the idea that the B version was written by John Trevisa, on the basis that he found similarities in words and expressions to the Cornish Miracle plays, of which only Trevisa would have been aware, from his days at Glasney Collegiate.

Towards the end of the fourteenth century, this poem would not have been accepted kindly by the church hierarchy, and if Trevisa were to have been involved, he would have wished to keep a low profile.

FINALE

There is much of Trevisa's life that we do not know. He says very little about his own life other than mentioning travelling to 'Aix le Chapel and Saxony but not to Rome'. He does not say with whom or give the purpose of these visits. He does not make any comments about the issues of his time, the wars with France, the peasants' revolt, the recurrent plagues, and the papal schism of 1378.

Did Trevisa translate a Bible into Cornish? He had all the necessary materials during his three-year absence from Queen's College, but when translation of the Bible into any vernacular was banned, he could have abandoned or maybe hidden it.

We do not know how Trevisa died. A new name appears as vicar of Berkeley in 1402, so we presume that this was the time of his death. When Archbishop Arundel returned to power under Henry IV, many writers who had been critical of the church had to redact their works. In the case of Chaucer, who had lampooned the clergy, there is strong evidence, as given by Terry Jones in his book *Who Murdered Chaucer?*, that he was murdered after examination.

Did Trevisa suffer a similar fate because of his translations and Lollard sympathies? It seems unlikely, as his sponsor, Lord Berkeley, was on good terms with the new king Henry IV.

In view of Trevisa's involvement in the Bible translation, it is ironic that 150 years after his death, the imposition of an English prayer book on a recusant Cornish speaking populace should bring about an uprising which caused many Cornish deaths and accelerated the demise of the Cornish language.

BIBLIOGRAPHY

The Life and Times of John Trevisa Medieval Scholar, David Fowler

John Trevisa, the Translator of Wycliffe B. A Consideration of the Evidence, W. R. Cooper

John Trevisa and the Use of English, Ronald Waldron

Clerical Discourse and Lay Audience in Late Medieval England, Fiona Somerset

Instruction and Information in the Works of John Trevisa, Jennifer Barton

Proponents of the view that Edward II escaped from Berkeley:

Edward II The Unconventional King, Kathryn Warner

The Greatest Traitor and *The Perfect King, Edward III,* Ian Mortimer

Isabella, Alison Weir

Sir Thomas Berkeley and his Patronage, Ralph Hanna

Who Murdered Chaucer? Terry Jones

Berkeley Epithets coined by John Smyth (1567-1640) of Nibley

Printed in the United States
By Bookmasters